MASSACHUSETTS

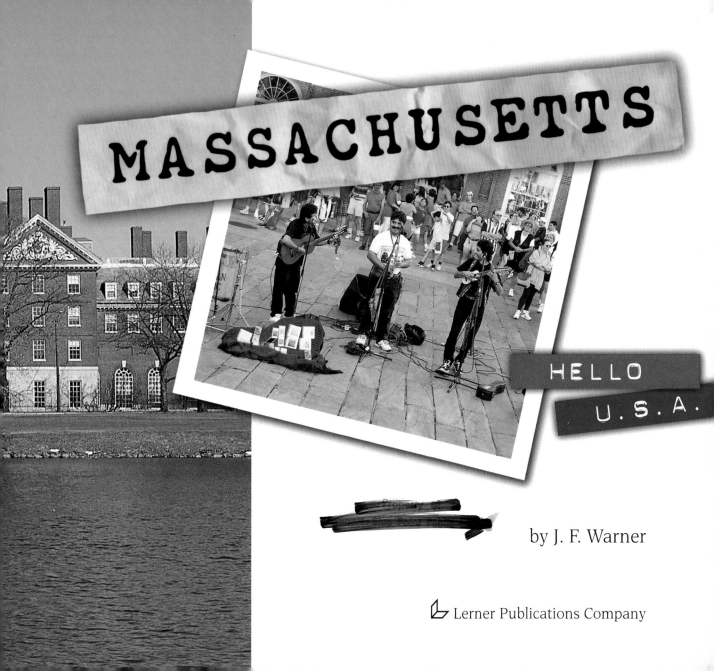

MASSACHUSETTS

HELLO U.S.A.

by J. F. Warner

Lerner Publications Company

You'll find this picture of sugar maple leaves at the beginning of each chapter in this book. Sugar maples are just one kind of tree in Massachusetts that changes color in the fall. From mid-September to late October, Massachusettans and visitors alike enjoy a spectacular show of fall color while driving through the state's forests.

Cover (left): Boston skyline. Cover (right): Nauset Light in Eastham, on Cape Cod. Pages 2-3: Crew teams on the Charles River in Cambridge. Page 3: Quincy Market in Boston.

This book is available in two editions:
Library binding by Lerner Publications Company, a division of Lerner Publishing Group
Soft cover by First Avenue Editions, an imprint of Lerner Publishing Group
241 First Avenue North
Minneapolis, MN 55401 U.S.A.

Website address: www.lernerbooks.com

LIBRARY OF CONGRESS CATALOGING-IN-PUBLICATION DATA

Warner, J. F. (John F.)
    Massachusetts / J. F. Warner (Revised and expanded 2nd edition)
      p. cm. — (Hello U.S.A.)
    Includes index.
    ISBN 0-8225-4050-9 (lib. bdg.: alk paper)
    ISBN 0-8225-4158-0 (pbk.)
    1. Massachusetts—Juvenile literature. 2. Massachusetts—Geography—Juvenile
literature. I. Title. II. Series.
F64.3.W37 2002
974.4—dc21   00-067789

Manufactured in the United States of America
1 2 3 4 5 6 – JR – 07 06 05 04 03 02

CONTENTS

On a western Massachusetts farm, horses graze in the sun.

THE LAND

The Bay State

assachusetts is a small state. In fact 70 states the size of Massachusetts could fit inside Alaska, the country's largest state. But Massachusetts makes up for its size with a great variety of landscapes and natural attractions.

Massachusetts is bordered on the north by Vermont and New Hampshire. New York lies to the west, while Connecticut and Rhode Island share the southern border. To the east, beyond Massachusetts Bay, is the Atlantic Ocean. The many bays along the Atlantic coast of Massachusetts have earned the state its nickname—the Bay State.

Thousands of years ago, powerful masses of moving ice called **glaciers** helped form the landscape of what later became Massachusetts.

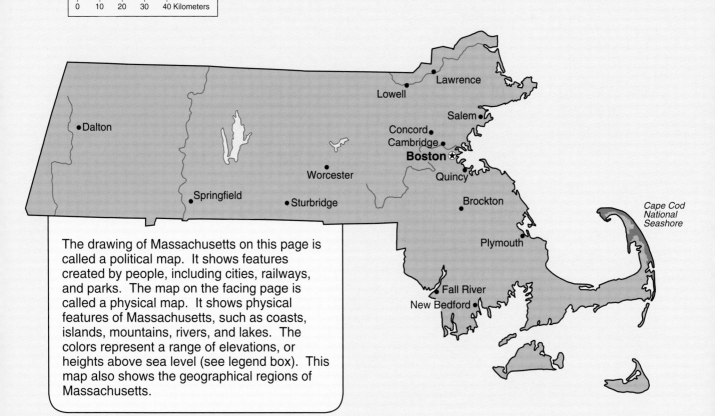

N
W ✦ E
S

Lawrence

Lowell

Salem

Concord
Cambridge

Dalton

Boston ⭐

Worcester

Quincy

Springfield

Sturbridge

Brockton

Plymouth

Cape Cod
National
Seashore

Fall River

New Bedford

The drawing of Massachusetts on this page is called a political map. It shows features created by people, including cities, railways, and parks. The map on the facing page is called a physical map. It shows physical features of Massachusetts, such as coasts, islands, mountains, rivers, and lakes. The colors represent a range of elevations, or heights above sea level (see legend box). This map also shows the geographical regions of Massachusetts.

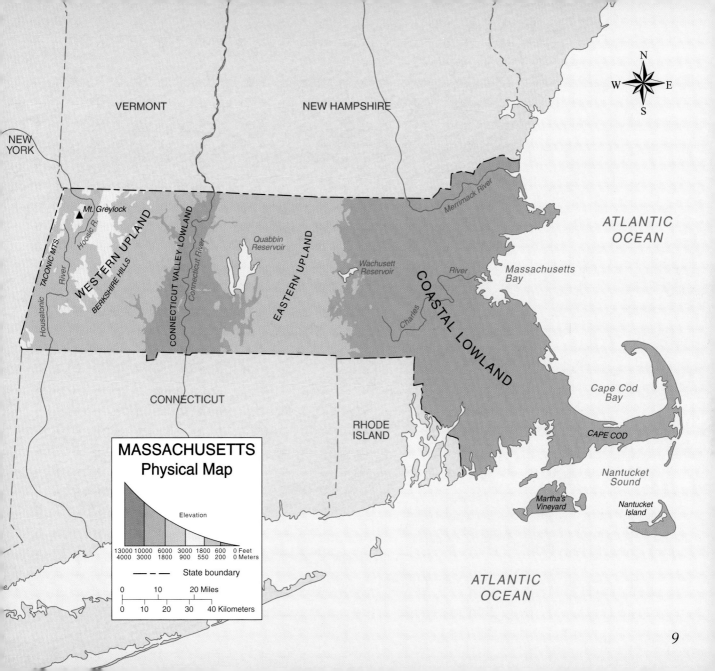

N
W E
S

VERMONT

NEW HAMPSHIRE

NEW YORK

ATLANTIC OCEAN

Mt. Greylock

TACONIC MTS.

Hoosic R.

WESTERN UPLAND

Housatonic River

BERKSHIRE HILLS

CONNECTICUT VALLEY LOWLAND

Connecticut River

Quabbin Reservoir

EASTERN UPLAND

Wachusett Reservoir

Merrimack River

Massachusetts Bay

River

COASTAL LOWLAND

Charles

CONNECTICUT

RHODE ISLAND

Cape Cod Bay

CAPE COD

Nantucket Sound

Martha's Vineyard

Nantucket Island

ATLANTIC OCEAN

MASSACHUSETTS
Physical Map

Elevation

| 13000 | 10000 | 6000 | 3000 | 1800 | 600 | 0 Feet |
| 4000 | 3000 | 1800 | 900 | 550 | 200 | 0 Meters |

- - - State boundary

0   10   20 Miles
0   10   20   30   40 Kilometers

As they slowly traveled across the region, the glaciers scraped the tops of mountains and dumped rocks, clay, and sand in low-lying areas. The glaciers also left rolling hills called **drumlins.** The drumlins are part of the Coastal Lowland—one of Massachusetts's four main land regions. Glaciers also shaped the valleys and hills of Massachusetts's other regions—the Eastern Upland, the Connecticut Valley Lowland, and the Western Upland.

The Coastal Lowland stretches inland from the seashore. Hundreds of small lakes and ponds dot this region, where pitch pines and scrub oaks grow. Sandy beaches line Massachusetts Bay and Cape Cod, a narrow **peninsula** that juts into the Atlantic Ocean. Across Nantucket Sound lie Nantucket, Martha's Vineyard, and smaller islands.

Families collect rocks and seashells at Cape Cod National Seashore.

Azaleas grow well in the Eastern Upland.

The land rises to elevations of 1,000 feet and higher in the Eastern Upland. Streams have cut narrow valleys through the hills of this region, which covers about half of Massachusetts. Stands of birch, beech, and pine trees thrive here, along with flowers such as marsh marigolds, bloodroots, and azaleas.

To the west, the land gradually slopes downward to the narrow Connecticut Valley Lowland. This region follows the banks of the Connecticut River. The soil here is fertile, making the Connecticut Valley an important agricultural region. Farmers in the valley raise fruit, corn, and livestock.

Livestock *(above)* and many types of crops *(right)* thrive in the Connecticut Valley Lowland.

In the fall, red and yellow sugar maple leaves brighten the landscape.

The Western Upland stretches from the Connecticut Valley Lowland to the bordering state of New York. Within the Western Upland are the Taconic Mountains and the Berkshire Hills. Mount Greylock, the highest spot in Massachusetts, rises 3,491 feet in the Berkshire Hills.

Several major rivers—including the Connecticut, the Charles, the Merrimack, the Housatonic, and the Hoosic—flow through Massachusetts. At several places, river dams have been built to collect water in **reservoirs** (artificial lakes). Two of the largest reservoirs—Quabbin and Wachusett—supply drinking water to the city of Boston.

The climate of Massachusetts is typical of the northeastern United States. Summers are usually warm and humid. Both rain and snow fall in the winter. But the weather varies from one region of Massachusetts to the next.

During the winter, mild ocean winds blow inland, raising temperatures in the Coastal Lowland. This region is also the warmest during the summer, while the Eastern Upland is the coolest. The Western Upland, the farthest region from the sea, is the coldest during the winter.

The island of Martha's Vineyard is a popular destination for tourists during the warm, sunny summers.

Bobcats *(above)* prowl the snow-covered fields and forests of Massachusetts *(right)* during the winter.

January temperatures in the state average 25° F. In July the average is 71° F. The lowest temperature ever recorded was −34° F, and the highest was 107° F. Rainfall, which is generally heavier in the east, ranges from 38 to 48 inches. The mountains of western Massachusetts receive the most snow— up to 75 inches a year.

Plentiful **precipitation** (rain, snow, sleet, and hail) allows thick forests to thrive in many parts of the state. Birch, beech, maple, and oak trees grow in the uplands, while pines and other evergreen trees are common along the coast. Marsh grasses favor the sandy soil of the Coastal Lowland.

The forests of Massachusetts are home to many animals. Rabbits, bobcats, deer, and foxes roam the uplands. The streams of the Western Upland shelter muskrat and beavers. Birds such as pheasant and partridge nest in fields and forests throughout the state. The beaches and harbors of the Atlantic coast attract terns, gulls, and other seabirds.

Freedom and Industry

Native American peoples, or Indians, have lived in the area that later became Massachusetts for at least 3,000 years. The Algonquians, a group of many different Native American nations, settled much of eastern North America. Algonquian peoples in Massachusetts included the Nipmuc, Nauset, Pennacook, and Wampanoag.

The Algonquians hunted deer and beavers and grew crops—including corn, beans, and squash—in fertile land near rivers. They built canoes from birch bark and sewed their clothing from buckskin (deer hides). Algonquian homes, called wigwams, had frames made of strong wooden poles, which were covered by bark or animal skins. The wigwams provided warm shelter during the winter.

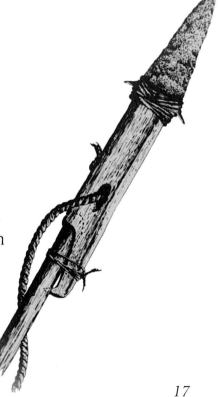

Wigwams *(right)* served as homes for the Algonquians. Deer provided meat and hides. To hunt deer *(below right)*, one group of hunters chased the animals into a space where two hedges, or fences, came together. The deer were trapped at the narrow end. There, another group of hunters waited with bows and arrows to end the chase.

The Pilgrims took 65 days to cross the Atlantic Ocean in the *Mayflower*.

The lives of the Algonquian peoples changed in the early 1600s, when European sea captains began exploring the shores of Cape Cod and the mainland of Massachusetts. The Europeans brought with them deadly diseases, such as smallpox, that killed thousands of Indians along the Atlantic coast.

In 1620 a group of 102 people left Great Britain. Called **Pilgrims,** they were seeking the freedom to establish their own church. They boarded the *Mayflower* and set sail for Virginia, a British **colony** (settlement) along the Atlantic coast of North America.

After a long sea voyage, the *Mayflower* strayed off course and anchored off the shores of Cape Cod.

A small landing party went ashore to explore the peninsula. They found that the soil was too poor to farm. The *Mayflower* later sailed across Cape Cod Bay.

The settlers landed on the western shore of the bay. There they found good soil, plentiful game, and a safe harbor. The *Mayflower*'s passengers decided to stay and build a new colony, which they named Plymouth.

The Pilgrims were hardworking, but they knew

The first winters in Plymouth Colony were cold, snowy, and difficult for the new settlers.

little about farming and were unprepared for their new life at Plymouth Colony. Fewer than 60 of the settlers survived the first winter, partly because they did not store enough food. Without the help of two Native Americans, Samoset and Squanto, the colony probably would have failed.

Squanto taught the Pilgrims how to plant corn, where to fish and hunt, and which plants were safe to use as food or medicine. Samoset introduced the Pilgrims to Massasoit, the sachem (great chief) of the Wampanoag Indians.

Soon after their first meeting, Massasoit and the Pilgrims signed a peace **treaty** (agreement) that would last more than 50 years. The Pilgrims and the Wampanoag promised not to harm each other. Anyone breaking the treaty would be sent to their own people for punishment.

To thank the Indians for their help, the Pilgrims invited them to a harvest feast. The feast, held in November 1621, marked the Pilgrims' first anniversary at Plymouth. The celebration lasted three days and became the first Thanksgiving in America.

At Samoset's first meeting with the Pilgrims in 1621, he surprised them by speaking English. British fishers had taught him their language when he met them on the coast of what later became Maine.

During the 1620s, new settlers arrived in Plymouth Colony. Some moved on to begin smaller settlements in Quincy, Salem, and Watertown. In 1630 a group of **Puritans** led by John Winthrop arrived in Salem. Like the Pilgrims, the Puritans were seeking religious freedom.

The British king had given the Puritans permission to begin a new colony near Plymouth. Soon after landing in Salem, the Puritans founded the city of Boston, which became the capital of their colony—Massachusetts Bay Colony. Near Boston, some of the newcomers founded Harvard, the oldest college in North America. The colony grew at a rate of 1,000 settlers a year for the next 10 years.

John Winthrop *(center, in hat)* was elected governor of Massachusetts Bay Colony before the Puritans set sail for America.

British colonists called Metacomet King Philip. He was killed in a battle against settlers in 1676.

The success of the Puritans, however, became the misfortune of the Native Americans. The Puritans seized land without paying for it, and they made Indians obey the strict Puritan laws. As early as 1637, fighting broke out between the Puritans and the Wampanoag.

The conflict over land led to King Philip's War, which broke out in 1675. After several bloody battles, the war ended in the defeat of the Wampanoag and in the death of their leader, Metacomet. With much of their land occupied by European settlers, the Wampanoag fled.

At the same time, thousands of new settlers arrived to work on the ships and in the harbors of Plymouth and Massachusetts Bay. As their economies grew, the people of the two colonies found that they had common interests and goals. In 1691 the British king and queen, William and Mary, allowed them to form a new colony called Massachusetts, which combined the colonies of Plymouth and Massachusetts Bay.

Trouble Brews in Salem

In 1692 Salem Village was a quiet rural community near the busy port of Salem. But late in the year, strange events began happening in the village. Frightened by tales of West Indian voodoo, several young women began to suffer frightening fits and visions. Suspecting that witchcraft was at work, the young women accused a West Indian woman in Salem of casting spells on them.

Soon the entire village was taking sides in the case. Samuel Parris, a minister from Salem Village, led the witch-hunt. Parris and his followers accused dozens of people of practicing witchcraft. Even the wife of William Phips, the governor of the colony, came under suspicion.

A special court in Salem convicted and hanged 19 people as witches. Giles Corey, a man who refused to plead either innocent or guilty, was pressed to death with heavy stones. A total of 150 people went to jail. But soon the people of Massachusetts turned against the witch trials, realizing that the accusations were false. In October, Governor Phips ended the trials and released all suspected witches from prison.

During the 1700s, Britain forced the colonists in North America to pay heavy taxes to support the British army. Angered, some people in Massachusetts called for independence from Britain. But the British earned a lot of money from their colonies and did not want to give them up. To maintain order, the British government sent soldiers to Massachusetts.

Protests in Massachusetts and in other North American colonies grew violent. On March 5, 1770, a squad of British Redcoats (soldiers named for their bright red uniforms) opened fire on a crowd in Boston. Five colonists were killed. The colonists called this event the Boston Massacre.

British soldiers fire on a crowd during the Boston Massacre. This picture inspired many people to rebel against British rule.

The Boston Tea Party took place on a cold December night in 1773. To protest the high taxes the British put on tea, colonists dressed as Indians boarded three British ships in Boston Harbor and dumped hundreds of crates of tea into the water.

In 1773 several citizens of Boston dumped 343 chests of British tea into Boston Harbor. After this event, called the Boston Tea Party, the British sent more troops and passed laws to punish the colonists.

In 1775 volunteer soldiers from the colonies clashed with the British army in the Massachusetts towns of Concord and Lexington. When they fired on the British troops, the colonists sparked the American Revolution. The next year, 13 of Britain's North American colonies, including Massachusetts, declared their independence.

The True Story of the Midnight Ride

By 1775 the colony of Massachusetts was ready to fight the British. Determined to keep control, the British general Thomas Gage ordered his forces to march on the Massachusetts towns of Lexington and Concord. On April 18, 700 British Redcoats set out from Boston.

A Boston silversmith named Paul Revere found out about the mission and decided to act. At 10:00 that night, Revere and a friend, William Dawes, set out for Lexington to warn rebel leaders that the British were coming. At midnight the two men reached Lexington, where Dr. Samuel Prescott joined them. But before Revere and Dawes could reach Concord, the British arrested the two men. Only Dr. Prescott made it past the British patrols.

Thanks to Samuel Prescott, the rebels at Concord were ready for the Redcoats. But Prescott was forgotten after Henry Wadsworth Longfellow, a Massachusetts writer, penned "Paul Revere's Ride" in 1863. Because of Longfellow's poem, the Boston silversmith—not Samuel Prescott—went down in history as the hero of the midnight ride.

In Cambridge, Massachusetts, General George Washington took command of the colonial forces, known as the Continental Army. In 1776 Washington forced British troops out of Boston. He led the Continental Army until 1783, when Britain agreed to a peace treaty and withdrew the Redcoats from the colonies.

The colonists then formed their own country—the United States of America. They wrote a **constitution** that explained how the new government would work. When Massachusetts approved the Constitution of the United States in 1788, it became the sixth state to join the new union.

One year later, General Washington became the nation's first president. Voters elected John Adams of Massachusetts as the second president in 1796. John Quincy Adams, his son, would become the sixth president in 1825.

As the country grew, so did shipping in Massachusetts. Trading ships carried the state's goods to nations all over the world. Whaling ships also sailed from the ports of New Bedford and Fall River.

Hunting enormous whales on the high seas could be very dangerous, but the profits were great.

Whalers hunted the animals for their fat, which was made into a valuable lamp oil. In the early 1800s, France and other European countries became important trading partners for Massachusetts.

At the same time, Britain and the United States were in conflict. Britain, which was at war with France, was trying to prevent Americans from trading with the French. The British were also searching U.S. ships and forcing U.S. sailors into the British navy. This led to war between the United States and Britain in 1812.

Although it ended quickly, the War of 1812 prevented Massachusetts from buying or selling its goods in Europe. As a result, the state had to start making more of its own products. It soon became a pioneer in manufacturing.

In 1814 Francis Cabot Lowell built a cotton mill in the town of Waltham. The new textile mill was the first in the United States to combine all the operations needed to turn raw cotton into finished cloth. After Lowell's death, his business partners built an entire city of mills—called Lowell—on the banks of the Merrimack River north of Boston.

The efforts of Francis Cabot Lowell helped make Massachusetts a leader in manufacturing.

Companies in Lowell and in other Massachusetts cities made clothing, shoes, furniture, artificial limbs, musical instruments, and clipper ships. People seeking good wages and a better life moved from farms into the cities to work in the new factories.

As the state's economy grew, **immigrants** from poor European countries arrived to look for jobs. Between 1846 and 1856, more than 1,000 Irish newcomers settled in Boston every month. By 1860 the state's population had topped 1 million.

The textile (cloth) mills of Massachusetts provided jobs for many newcomers from Europe.

The House on Walden Pond

In 1845 a young writer from Concord named Henry David Thoreau began making plans to build a house. The house would be small and plain, but it would satisfy his need for shelter and comfort. Thoreau decided to build the house on the shores of Walden Pond, on the outskirts of Concord.

Thoreau wrote about his experience in *Walden; or, Life in the Woods*. In the book, he claimed that modern, fast-paced society made people unhappy, even desperate. But the simple life at Walden Pond offered something different—peace of mind. *Walden* has fascinated millions of readers since it first appeared in 1854.

With a growing audience for newspapers and books, publishing boomed in Massachusetts. William Lloyd Garrison of Boston produced a newspaper called *The Liberator.* In his articles, Garrison called for an end to slavery, a common practice in Southern states. (Massachusetts had outlawed slavery in 1783.) Garrison and many citizens of Massachusetts and other Northern states helped runaway slaves escape from the South.

Massachusetts sent more than 145,000 soldiers to fight for the United States during the Civil War.

In 1861 conflicts between the Southern slaveholding states and the Northern free states led to the Civil War. The industries of the North became an important part of the war effort. Massachusetts supplied Northern troops with ships, clothing, and weapons. In addition, more than 14,000 soldiers from Massachusetts were killed or wounded while fighting for the North. The South surrendered in 1865.

After the war, industry continued to grow in Massachusetts. Immigrants from Italy, Portugal, Germany, Poland, and many other countries worked in the mills and factories. But the workdays were long and the pay was low. Many workers earned only 85 cents for a 12-hour day. Women and children usually earned even less.

To improve these conditions, many laborers joined **unions** (workers' organizations) in the early 1900s. When a union called a strike, the workers stayed home from their jobs. The strikes forced business owners to either pay better wages or shut down their factories. The unions also persuaded Massachusetts to pass new laws controlling the hours and pay for workers.

Police try to control striking workers in Lawrence, Massachusetts, in 1912.

A Sticky Situation

On January 15, 1919, one of the strangest floods in history nearly destroyed the city of Boston. That was the day of the Great Molasses Flood. A huge steel tank holding more than 2 million gallons of molasses suddenly burst. The sweet, sticky wave poured through the city, destroying everything in its path.

When the flood of molasses finally came to a halt, a layer of goo three feet thick covered much of Boston. In all, 21 people died in the flood, and at least 50 more were badly hurt. The smell of molasses lasted for months. Some people claim that, on hot days, the scent of molasses still lingers in the Boston air.

Because factory workers earned such low wages during the early 1900s, they could afford to live only in crowded, dirty neighborhoods.

During World War I (1914–1918), factories in Massachusetts turned out supplies for the U.S. armed forces. But the state's economy slumped in the 1920s. Massachusetts's companies could not compete with Southern businesses, which paid workers lower wages in order to make and sell goods more cheaply. As a result, Massachusetts had a hard time selling its higher-priced products. Many factories closed, and thousands of workers lost their jobs.

Conditions worsened during the Great Depression, which began in 1929. This economic crisis forced thousands of companies and banks throughout the nation to go out of business. In the worst years of the depression, almost half of all workers in Massachusetts were jobless.

The economy improved when the United States entered World War II in 1941. Factories in Massachusetts again supplied weapons, and the state's shipyards built military vessels. But after the war ended in 1945, many of the state's remaining shoe and textile companies moved to the South.

At the same time, scientists in Massachusetts were developing computers and other new products. In the 1950s and 1960s, high-tech electronics companies started up near Boston. Researchers and engineers at the Massachusetts Institute of Technology (MIT) and other universities in the Boston area played an important part in the explosion of high-tech industry. The industry grew rapidly and created thousands of well-paying jobs.

Massachusetts continues to attract newcomers who seek a college education or who work in high-tech and manufacturing industries. The state's famous universities are training future engineers, computer designers, and business owners. With its talented workforce, Massachusetts has a promising future.

Massachusetts women served their country during World War II by making weapons for the war effort.

PEOPLE & ECONOMY

A Rich Heritage

eople from all over the world have come to Massachusetts throughout its long history. Seeking religious freedom, the first British colonists built farms and ports near the seacoast. In the 1800s, Italian, Irish, and Portuguese immigrants worked on fishing boats or in factories. People of European descent currently make up nearly 90 percent of the state's population of 6.3 million people.

This 200-year-old windmill on Nantucket Island is one of many historical sites in Massachusetts.

Before the Civil War, African Americans came to Massachusetts to escape slavery. They make up about 6 percent of the state's population. About the same number of Latinos, who come from Mexico and Central and South America, live in Massachusetts. Asian Americans, many of whom arrived after World War II, make up about 4 percent of the state's population. Native Americans, the area's first people, number only about 15,000—fewer than 1 percent.

Kids in Worcester, Massachusetts, take a break on a summer day.

Massachusettans gather for music and fun at Faneuil Hall in Boston.

About 8 out of every 10 residents of Massachusetts live in cities. Boston, the capital city, is the state's business and education center. Worcester, in central Massachusetts, and Springfield in the west are home to factories that produce machinery, textiles, and other manufactured goods. On Buzzards Bay, west of Cape Cod, lies the fishing port of New Bedford.

Boston at night

Although Boston continues to grow rapidly, many of the city's historical sites have been carefully preserved. Colonial mansions still line the bumpy brick streets of Beacon Hill. A two-story wooden house in the North End was once the home of Paul Revere, who warned colonists of a British invasion in 1775. Along the Black Heritage Trail are the homes, schools, and churches of African American Bostonians from the 1800s.

The USS *Constitution* earned its nickname, "Old Ironsides," during the War of 1812. Cannonballs bounced off its sides, as if the ship were made of iron.

At the Charlestown Navy Yard, visitors tour the USS *Constitution*, the oldest warship in the U.S. Navy. Bostonians can relax and picnic on Boston Common—the nations's first public park—or see dolphins, sharks, and sea turtles at the New England Aquarium.

Massachusetts has preserved hundreds of its historic places. Plymouth Rock marks the site where the Pilgrims landed in 1620. The first battles of the American Revolution were fought at Lexington and at the Old North Bridge in Concord. Factories and mills in Lowell show the workings of a manufacturing town as it was in the early 1800s.

Outdoor enthusiasts enjoy hiking and camping in Massachusetts's forests, which cover nearly three-fifths of the state. Every summer swimmers and sunbathers escape to Cape Cod National Seashore. It has 43,000 acres of sand dunes, beaches, woodlands, and marshes. Adventuresome hikers follow the Appalachian Trail, which winds through the mountains of western Massachusetts on its way from Maine to Georgia.

Sea Gull Beach in West Yarmouth is a popular spot for sunbathers.

As the birthplace of basketball, Massachusetts boasts the Boston Celtics. The Celtics and the Boston Bruins, a professional hockey team, play their games at FleetCenter in Boston. Fenway Park, one of the country's oldest baseball stadiums, has been the home of the Boston Red Sox since 1912. The team has plans to build a new ballpark, but many fans hope the old one will be restored.

The New England Patriots meet their professional football opponents in Foxboro, a few miles south of Boston. Every other year at Cambridge, Harvard University plays Yale University, a longtime football rival from Connecticut.

Students in Massachusetts benefit from an excellent educational system. Harvard, the nation's oldest university, is considered by many scholars to be one of the best in the world.

A Boston Red Sox batter gets ready for a pitch.

Future engineers and scientists study at MIT, a leading high-tech university that is also in Cambridge. College students in the town of Amherst attend Amherst College or the University of Massachusetts.

People of many ages attend school in Massachusetts. An elementary school student *(inset)* takes time from school to play. A college crew team *(above)* practices at Harvard University in Cambridge.

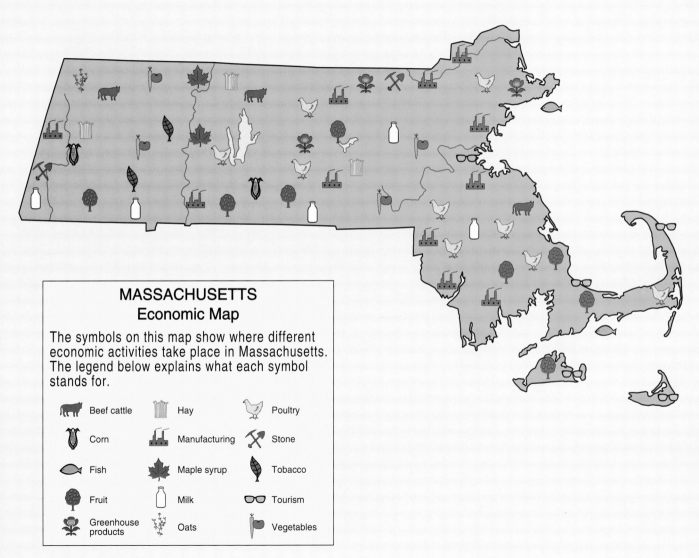

MASSACHUSETTS
Economic Map

The symbols on this map show where different economic activities take place in Massachusetts. The legend below explains what each symbol stands for.

Beef cattle		Hay		Poultry	
Corn		Manufacturing		Stone	
Fish		Maple syrup		Tobacco	
Fruit		Milk		Tourism	
Greenhouse products		Oats		Vegetables	

Cranberries are harvested on Cape Cod.

Many college graduates remain in Massachusetts to pursue their careers. Most of the state's workers —71 percent—have jobs helping other people or businesses. These service workers include doctors, teachers, lawyers, and bank tellers. The tourism industry earns Massachusetts about $11 billion a year. It employs hotel workers, travel agents, and tour guides. The state draws about 27 million visitors each year. Government workers make up about 11 percent of Massachusetts's workforce.

About 15 percent of Massachusetts's workers have jobs in manufacturing. Some factory workers still make shoes and fabrics. Others assemble machinery, sew clothing, process paper, or craft musical instruments. Workers at printing houses produce books, magazines, and newspapers. Skilled high-tech employees manufacture computers and robots.

While agriculture and fishing still earn money for Massachusetts, only 1 percent of the state's workers farm or fish. Massachusetts's farmers raise vegetables and dairy products and harvest about half of all the cranberries in the United States.

An old fishing boat gets some repairs and a new coat of paint.

Fishing companies in Massachusetts haul in scallops, cod, haddock, and perch from the Atlantic Ocean. The largest fishing fleets sail from the ports of New Bedford and Gloucester.

But the state's fishing industry is growing smaller every year. Fishing companies are finding it more and more expensive to operate their fleets. In addition, some kinds of fish are fast disappearing because fishers have caught too many. Other fish have been poisoned by wastes dumped into rivers and harbors. Because of pollution, the state has placed restrictions on commercial fishing boats working in Boston Harbor, in Massachusetts Bay, and in other areas.

Massachusetts is a major producer of scallops.

THE ENVIRONMENT

Cleaning Up Boston Harbor

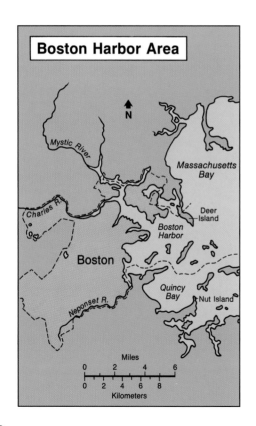

Boston Harbor Area

Mystic River

Massachusetts Bay

Charles R.

Deer Island

Boston Harbor

Boston

Quincy Bay

Nut Island

Neponset R.

Miles
0 2 4 6

0 2 4 6 8
Kilometers

Boston Harbor extends five miles out to Massachusetts Bay. The harbor has been an important part of Boston's economy for more than 300 years. But the rapid growth of the city has caused serious water pollution. Much more than tea has ended up in Boston Harbor, which was once one of the most polluted waterways in the United States.

Boston Harbor plays a vital role in Massachusetts's economy.

Boston Harbor businesses depend on the money tourists spend in the area.

For many years, untreated sewage from Boston's homes and factories ran directly into the harbor's waters. Several rivers, including the Charles, the Mystic, and the Neponset, carried pollutants from other cities into the harbor.

In the mid-1900s, Boston built two sewage-treatment plants to remove poisonous bacteria from wastewater. But the plants were unable to handle the rising flow of sewage. By the 1970s, more than 500 million gallons of poorly treated wastewater were flowing into the harbor every day.

Polluted water flows into Boston Harbor from the Charles River.

The bad-smelling water drove recreational boaters from the harbor. Tourists avoided the waterfront, and swimmers stayed away from the filthy beaches, where untreated sewage was washing ashore. The polluted water also made the harbor's fish poisonous to eat. As many as 14,000 workers in the local fishing industry lost their jobs.

Old sewage-treatment plants on Deer Island *(above)* and Nut Island could not handle all the wastewater that flowed into Boston Harbor.

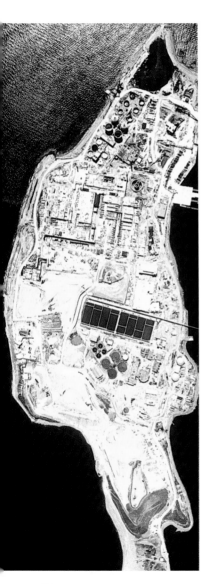

To solve the problem, state officials formed the Massachusetts Water Resources Authority (MWRA) in 1985. The MWRA stopped dumping untreated sewage into Boston Harbor in 1991. It improved old sewage-treatment plants and built a new one on Deer Island, near the mouth of Boston Harbor. The Deer Island plant opened in different stages in 1995, 1997, and 1999. In September 2000, officials opened a 9.5-mile outflow pipe that carries treated sewage from the plant out to Massachusetts Bay.

Workers built underwater tunnels *(above)* for the new sewage-treatment plant on Deer Island *(left)*.

As a result of these efforts, Boston Harbor is no longer one of the dirtiest harbors in America. Seals and porpoises have returned to the harbor. Fish and shellfish are less contaminated. It's usually safe to fish in the harbor and to swim at beaches.

However, the new treatment plant and the outflow pipe are not without some problems of their own.

The new sewage-treatment plant has made Boston Harbor cleaner and safer.

The harbor clean-up project costs over $4 billion. The state and federal governments would not pay for most of this, so much of the funding has come from citizens. Residents of some parts of Boston must pay very high sewer bills. Some people argue that the state should pay instead, since Boston Harbor is important to the economy of all of Massachusetts.

Also, some environmentalists worry that even treated sewage pollutes the waters of Massachusetts Bay. The bay is a feeding ground for endangered North Atlantic right and humpback whales. Others fear that it will hurt the beaches of Cape Cod.

Watercraft of all kinds sail the waters of Boston Harbor.

The harbor clean-up has so far been a success story, but new challenges face the people of Massachusetts. They have learned that ignoring environmental problems only makes them more difficult to solve. They are working to build on the progress they have made.

As clean-up efforts progress, Boston Harbor is becoming a safer place for people to swim, boat, and fish. These swimmers compete in a race across the harbor.

ALL ABOUT MASSACHUSETTS

Fun Facts

A small lake in Massachusetts has the longest name of any place in the United States. Webster Lake's original Nipmuc Indian name is Chargoggagoggmanchaugagogg-chaubunagungamaug, which means "You fish on your side of the lake, I fish on my side, and no one fishes in the middle."

Two popular sports had their beginnings in Massachusetts. In 1891 James Naismith of Springfield invented basketball, creating a team sport that could be played indoors during the winter. In 1895 William Morgan of Holyoke invented volleyball.

Massachusetts takes its name from the Massachuset Indians, who once lived a few miles south of what became Boston in an area known as Blue Hill. The tribe's name means "great hill."

During the 1600s, Massachusetts Puritans made it a crime to celebrate Christmas, to dance at weddings, to perform religious music, to put on plays, and to wear buttons, lace, or shoe buckles.

American paper money is printed on paper made from a secret formula at the Crane and Company mill in Dalton, Massachusetts.

Opposite page: Physical education teacher James Naismith shows how to hold one of the first basketballs.

STATE SONG

The state song of Massachusetts was written by Arthur J. Marsh, who lived in Wellesley, Massachusetts. In 1966 it became the unofficial state song, and in 1981 the state legislature made it the official state song.

ALL HAIL TO MASSACHUSETTS

Words and music by Arthur J. Marsh

All hail to Mas-sa-chu-setts, the land of the free and the brave! For Bun-ker Hill and Charles-town and flag we love to wave: For Lex-ing-ton and Con - cord and the shot heard round the world: All hail to Mas-sa-chu - setts we'll keep her flag un-furled. She stands up-right for free-dom's light that shines from sea to sea: All hail to Mas-sa-chu - setts! Our coun-try 'tis of thee!

You can hear "All Hail to Massachusetts" by visiting this website:
<http://www.50states.com/songs/mass.htm>

A MASSACHUSETTS RECIPE

Whitman, Massachusetts, is the birthplace of the chocolate chip cookie. Ruth and Kenneth Wakefield ran the Toll House Inn in Whitman. In 1930 Mrs. Wakefield added chopped-up pieces of a chocolate bar to traditional cookie dough. Her cookies were so tasty and successful that in 1939 the Nestlé candy company began selling ready-made bits of chocolate. This popular recipe still bears the name of Mrs. Wakefield's Massachusetts inn.

ORIGINAL NESTLÉ® TOLL HOUSE® CHOCOLATE CHIP COOKIE RECIPE

Ask an adult to preheat the oven to 375° F.

2¼ cups all-purpose flour
1 teaspoon baking soda
1 teaspoon salt
1 cup (2 sticks, ½ pound) butter, softened
¾ cup granulated (white) sugar

¾ cup packed brown sugar
1 teaspoon vanilla extract
2 eggs
2 cups (12-ounce package) chocolate chips

1. Combine flour, baking soda, and salt in small bowl. Set aside.
2. Beat butter, granulated sugar, brown sugar, and vanilla in large mixer bowl.
3. Add eggs one at a time, beating the mixture well after each one. Gradually beat in flour-mixture. Stir in chocolate chips.
4. Using a spoon, drop rounded balls of dough onto ungreased baking sheets.
5. Ask an adult for help with the next steps. Bake the cookies in preheated oven for 9 to 11 minutes or until golden brown.
6. Let stand for 2 minutes; remove to wire racks to cool completely.

HISTORICAL TIMELINE

10,000 B.C.   Native Americans settle in the area of Massachusetts.

A.D. 1498   John Cabot sails along the coast of Massachusetts.

1620   Pilgrims arrive at Plymouth.

1636   Harvard becomes the first college in the colonies.

1675   Massachusetts colonists fight King Philip's War against the Wampanoag.

1689–1763   Massachusetts colonists help the British win the French and Indian Wars.

1691   British monarchs William and Mary grant a royal charter to the new colony of Massachusetts.

1692   The Salem Witchcraft Trials take place.

1770   British soldiers kill several colonists in the Boston Massacre.

1773   Colonists dump British tea into Boston Harbor during the Boston Tea Party.

1775 The American Revolution begins with battles at Lexington and Concord.

1780 Massachusetts adopts a state constitution.

1788 Massachusetts becomes the sixth state.

1814 Francis Cabot Lowell builds a modern cotton mill in Waltham

1820 Maine separates from Massachusetts and becomes a state.

1876 Alexander Graham Bell invents the telephone in Boston.

1912 Strikes force employers to improve conditions in Massachusetts's factories.

1974 Integration of Boston public schools is ordered by a federal court.

1980 New companies in the Boston area begin producing computers and biotechnology products.

2000 Officials open a new outflow pipe to carry treated sewage out of Boston Harbor to Massachusetts Bay.

OUTSTANDING MASSACHUSETTANS

John Adams

Abigail Adams (1744–1818) was born in Weymouth, Massachusetts. In 1764 she married John Adams, who later became the second president of the United States. She is known for asking her husband to "remember the ladies" in the new nation's laws.

John Adams (1735–1826) of Braintree (now Quincy), Massachusetts, was elected the second president of the United States in 1796. Adams was the first president to live in the White House in Washington, D.C.

Louisa May Alcott

Louisa May Alcott (1832–1888) moved with her family to Boston as a child. An author mainly of stories for young people, Alcott's most famous book is *Little Women*.

Susan B. Anthony (1820–1906) was a women's rights advocate born in Adams, Massachusetts. She fought hard to win women the right to vote, to control personal property, and to gain custody of their children after a divorce.

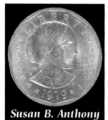

Susan B. Anthony

Crispus Attucks (1723?–1770), an African American resident of Boston, led a mob of colonists against a squad of British soldiers on March 5, 1770. Attucks was the first to fall as the Redcoats fired on the crowd.

Alexander Graham Bell

Alexander Graham Bell (1847–1922) was born in Scotland but later moved to Boston, where he opened a school for teachers of the deaf. In 1876 Bell became the first person to send his voice over an electric wire. In the same year, he patented the first telephone.

Leonard Bernstein (1918–1990) was a composer and orchestral conductor best known for his musicals *West Side Story* and *Candide*. Born in Lawrence, Massachusetts, Bernstein introduced thousands of people to classical music through his lectures and television specials.

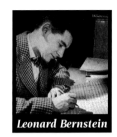

Leonard Bernstein

Patricia Bradley (born 1951) is one of the most successful professional golfers in history. Originally from Westford, Massachusetts, Bradley has won more than $5.5 million on the Ladies Professional Golf Association tour.

Patricia Bradley

Armando "Chick" Corea (born 1941) is a Grammy Award–winning musician from Chelsea, Massachusetts. A keyboard player and composer, Corea blends jazz, rock, classical, and other types of music in his performances.

Matt Damon (born 1970) grew up in Boston and attended Harvard University. Along with Ben Affleck, Damon won an Oscar and a Golden Globe for their screenplay for *Good Will Hunting*, in which Damon also starred.

Matt Damon

Bette Davis (1908–1989), a native of Lowell, starred in dozens of films, earning two Academy Awards. Davis's talent and strong personality helped create better film roles for women. Among her best-known movies are *Whatever Happened to Baby Jane?* and *All About Eve.*

Bette Davis

Fannie Farmer

Dr. Seuss

Robert Goddard

Oliver Wendell Holmes Jr.

William E. B. Du Bois (1868–1963) was a writer, educator, and civil rights leader. Born in Great Barrington, he attended Harvard University and later edited *Crisis*, the magazine of the National Association for the Advancement of Colored People (NAACP).

Fannie Farmer (1857–1915) was the first cook to use standard measurements in food recipes. She founded a cooking school and wrote *The Boston Cooking School Cook Book*. First published in 1896, this book later became the *Fannie Farmer Cookbook*.

Theodore Seuss Geisel (1904–1991), also known as Dr. Seuss, wrote easy-to-read rhyming books about make-believe creatures. Millions of children have enjoyed *The Cat in the Hat* and many other books by Dr. Seuss, who was born in Springfield.

Robert Goddard (1882–1945) dreamed of rockets, spacecraft, and trips to the moon as a young man. Raised in Worcester, he launched the world's first liquid-fuel rocket in 1926.

Oliver Wendell Holmes Jr. (1841–1935) practiced law in his hometown of Boston after serving in the Union army during the Civil War. Holmes served on the U.S. Supreme Court from 1902 until 1932 and became famous for teaching judges not to let their personal opinions influence their decisions in court.

Winslow Homer (1836–1910), an artist from Boston, taught himself to paint as a young man. He produced illustrations of the Civil War for the magazine *Harper's Weekly*. He later settled in Prouts Neck, Maine. Homer's best-known works are his seascapes.

John F. Kennedy (1917–1963), the 35th president of the United States, was born in Brookline, Massachusetts. The youngest president ever to be elected, he was assassinated in Dallas, Texas, on November 22, 1963.

John F. Kennedy

Jack Lemmon (born 1925), a well-known actor, was born in Boston. He starred in *The Odd Couple* and won Academy Awards for his work in *Mister Roberts* and *Save the Tiger*.

Edgar Allan Poe (1809–1849), who was born in Boston, wrote scary poems and stories that earned him a reputation as the nation's finest horror writer. His best-known stories include "The Tell-Tale Heart," "The Fall of the House of Usher," and the poem "The Raven."

Jack Lemmon

Sumner Redstone (born 1923) is the chairman of Viacom, Inc., a large entertainment company that owns Paramount Pictures, Blockbuster, and the cable channels MTV, Showtime, and Nickelodeon. A native of Boston, Redstone was the first theater operator to build multiplexes, where two or more movie screens operate under one roof.

Sumner Redstone

Ted Williams (born 1918) was one of the greatest hitters in baseball history. Born in San Diego, California, Williams spent 19 years playing for the Boston Red Sox. He hit 521 home runs and had a lifetime batting average of .344.

N. C. Wyeth (1882–1945) was an illustrator of children's novels. A native of Needham, Massachusetts, Wyeth used his great talent for drawing to illustrate books such as *Robin Hood* and *Treasure Island*.

Ted Williams

FACTS-AT-A-GLANCE

Nickname: Bay State

Song: "All Hail to Massachusetts"

Motto: Ense Petit Placidam Sub Libertate Quietem (By the Sword We Seek Peace, but Peace Only Under Liberty)

Flower: mayflower

Tree: American elm

Bird: black capped chickadee

Fish: cod

Insect: ladybug

Fossil: dinosaur tracks, found in Granby

Date and ranking of statehood: February 6, 1788, the sixth state

Capital: Boston

Area: 8,257 square miles

Rank in area, nationwide: 45th

Average January temperature: 25° F

Average July temperature: 71° F

Massachusetts has adopted several different flags during its long history. This state flag, which became official in 1971, features the state's coat of arms.

POPULATION GROWTH

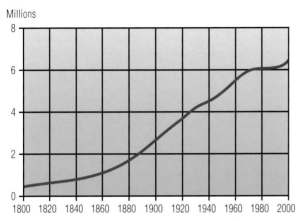

Millions

This chart shows how Massachusetts's population has grown from 1800 to 2000.

Massachusetts adopted its state seal in 1780, and it became official in 1885. The Latin words that appear on the seal mean "Seal of the Republic of Massachusetts."

Population: 6,349,097 (2000 census)

Rank in population, nationwide: 13th

Major cities and populations (2000 census): Boston (589,141), Worcester (172,648), Springfield (152,082), Lowell (105,167), New Bedford (93,768)

U.S. senators: 2

U.S. representatives: 10

Electoral votes: 12

Natural resources: granite, limestone, marble, natural harbors, peat, sand and gravel, sandstone, water

Agricultural products: apples, cranberries, greenhouse plants, vegetables, milk, eggs

Fishing industry: cod, flounder, scallops

Manufactured goods: electrical equipment and supplies, nonelectric machinery, scientific instruments, computers, transportation equipment, books and newspapers

WHERE MASSACHUSETTANS WORK

Services—71 percent (services include jobs in trade; community, social, and personal services; finance, insurance, and real estate; transportation, communication, and utilities)

Manufacturing—12 percent

Government—11 percent

Construction—5 percent

Agriculture and fishing—1 percent

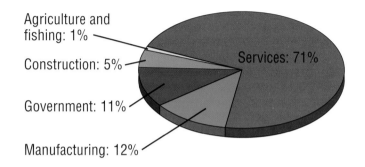

Agriculture and fishing: 1%

Construction: 5%

Government: 11%

Manufacturing: 12%

Services: 71%

GROSS STATE PRODUCT

Services—72 percent

Manufacturing—15 percent

Government—9 percent

Construction—3 percent

Agriculture and fishing—1 percent

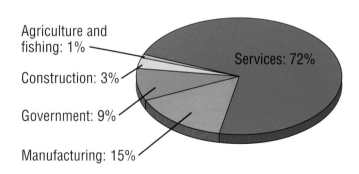

Agriculture and fishing: 1%

Construction: 3%

Government: 9%

Manufacturing: 15%

Services: 72%

MASSACHUSETTS WILDLIFE

Mammals: bat, beaver, bobcat, deer, fox, meadow mouse, muskrat, porcupine, rabbit, raccoon, skunk, squirrel, whales, woodchuck

Birds: gull, partridge, pheasant, tern

Reptiles: copperhead, timber rattlesnake

Fish: bass, clam, lobster, oyster, perch, pickerel, sunfish, trout

Trees: ash, beech, birch, eastern hemlock, eastern white and red pines, maple, pitch pine

Wild plants: azalea, dogwood, fern, marsh marigold, mayflower, mountain laurel, rhododendron, rush, sedge, skunk cabbage, Solomon's seal, trillium, viburnum, violet

PLACES TO VISIT

Basketball Hall of Fame, Springfield
Dr. James Naismith invented basketball in Springfield in 1891. The hall of fame includes a cinema and a fountain.

Black Heritage Trail, Boston
This trail winds through the Beacon Hill area of Boston, where black Bostonians of the 1800s lived. It includes sites that were part of the Underground Railroad.

Boston Common
Visitors can cruise the pond in swan boats and see statues inspired by the children's story *Make Way for Ducklings.*

Cape Cod National Seashore, Cape Cod
Stretching along the ocean from Chatham to Provincetown, this park features beaches, sand dunes, and forests.

Children's Museum and Museum of Science, Boston
At these museums, children of all ages make hands-on discoveries about science, history, cultural diversity, and themselves.

Harvard Square, Cambridge
America's oldest and most respected university is in a bustling historic and culturally rich neighborhood.

John Fitzgerald Kennedy National Historic Site, Brookline
The 35th president lived here from the time of his birth in 1917 until 1920.

Old Sturbridge Village, Sturbridge
This re-creation of an 1830s Massachusetts town allows visitors to learn about daily life at that time.

Old North Church, Boston
Before his famous ride in April 1775, Paul Revere saw two lanterns hanging in the steeple of Boston's oldest church.

Plimoth Plantation, Plymouth
This re-creation of a Pilgrim village features a ship modeled on the original *Mayflower.*

USS *Constitution* (Old Ironsides), Boston
A veteran of the War of 1812, the oldest commissioned ship in the U.S. Navy is docked in the Charlestown Navy Yard.

Walden Pond, Concord
Henry David Thoreau described his experiences here in his book *Walden.*

Whaling Museum, New Bedford
This museum devoted to the history of whaling features a model of a whaling ship and a skeleton of a whale.

Witch House, Salem
During the Salem witch hunts of 1692, over 200 accused witches were questioned in this house.

Old Ironsides on display in Boston

ANNUAL EVENTS

St. Patrick's Day Parade in Boston—*March*

Boston Marathon—*April*

Daffodil Festival on Nantucket Island—*April*

Whale Watch Cruises from Cape Ann to Cape Cod—*April–October*

Bunker Hill Day Weekend in Boston—*June*

Boston Chowderfest—*July*

Pilgrim Process Processional in Plymouth—*July–August*

Sandcastle Contest in Nantucket—*August*

Cranberry Harvest Festival in Harwich—*September*

Rowing Regatta in Cambridge—*October*

Chowder Contest on Martha's Vineyard—*December*

First Night Celebration in Boston—*New Year's Eve*

LEARN MORE ABOUT MASSACHUSETTS

BOOKS

General

Avakian, Monique. *A Historical Album of Massachusetts.* Brookfield, CT: The Millbrook Press, 1994.

Fradin, Dennis Brindell. *Massachusetts.* Chicago: Children's Press, 1991.

McNair, Sylvia. *Massachusetts.* Danbury, CT: Children's Press, 1998. For older readers.

Special Interest

Kent, Deborah. *Boston.* Danbury, CT: Children's Press, 1998. An introduction to Boston's sites, history, people, and culture.

Kent, Deborah. *Salem, Massachusetts.* Parsippany, NJ: Dillon Press, 1996. This book for middle readers describes the events leading up to and during the legendary witchcraft trials in Salem. It includes information about Salem after 1693 and historical sites to visit.

Longfellow, Henry Wadsworth. *Paul Revere's Ride.* New York: Dutton, 1990. Longfellow's classic account of Paul Revere's heroism is brought to life by Ted Rand's illustrations in this picture book.

Stein, R. Conrad. *The Pilgrims*. Chicago: Children's Press, 1995. With text and photographs, Stein introduces readers to the history of the Pilgrims and their effect on their new home in America.

Weidt, Maryann N. *Oh, the Places He Went: A Story about Dr. Seuss*. Minneapolis: Carolrhoda Books, 1994. Celebrated children's author Dr. Seuss (Theodore Seuss Geisel) grew up in Springfield, before gaining fame as a writer and illustrator.

Weidt, Maryann N. *Revolutionary Poet: A Story about Phillis Wheatley*. Minneapolis: Carolrhoda Books, 1997. Born in Africa and taken from her family at age seven, Phillis Wheatley was a slave in revolutionary Boston. She learned to read and write and later became an accomplished poet and the first black American to publish a book.

Fiction

Collier, Christopher, and James Lincoln Collier. *The Winter Hero*. New York: Four Winds Press, 1978. Teenager Justin Conkey struggles to understand his place in Shays' Rebellion, an uprising against the early government of Massachusetts.

Forbes, Esther. *Johnny Tremain*. Boston: Houghton Mifflin Company, 1998 (1943). After his hand is damaged in a silver-smithing accident, twelve-year-old Johnny must find other work. Winner of the 1943 Newbery Medal, this historical novel set in Boston takes readers through the events leading up to the Revolutionary War.

McCully, Emily Arnold. *The Bobbin Girl.* New York: Dial Books for Young Readers, 1996. In this picture book for young readers, ten-year-old Rebecca works in a mill in Lowell, Massachusetts, during the 1830s. She and her co-workers struggle for fair wages and decent working conditions.

WEBSITES

Official Website of the Commonwealth of Massachusetts
<http://www.state.ma.us>
The state's official website offers access to all kinds of information from state agencies.

Welcome to Massachusetts
<http://www.mass-vacation.com/index.shtml>
At the official website of the Massachusetts Office of Travel and Tourism, visitors can find out about all there is to see and do in the state, from watching whales to visiting Revolutionary War battlefields.

Boston Globe Online
<http://www.boston.com/globe>
The online version of the *Boston Globe*—Massachusetts's largest newspaper—covers national, state, and local news.

The History Place—JFK Photo History
<http://www.historyplace.com/kennedy/gallery.htm>
This site contains historical photographs of John F. Kennedy, who grew up in Massachusetts and later became the 35th president of the United States.

PRONUNCIATION GUIDE

Algonquian (al-GAHN-kwee-uhn)

Amherst (AM-erst)

Berkshire (BERK-sher)

Housatonic (hoo-suh-TAHN-ihk)

Massachuset (mass-uh-CHOO-suht)

Nipmuc (NIHP-muhk)

Pennacook (PEHN-uh-kook)

Quabbin (KWAH-bihn)

Samoset (SAM-uh-set)

Taconic (tuh-KAHN-ihk)

Wampanoag (wahm-puh-NOH-ag)

Worcester (WUS-ter)

GLOSSARY

colony: a territory ruled by a country some distance away

constitution: the system of basic laws or rules of a government, society, or organization; the document in which these laws or rules are written

drumlin: a hill of rocks and earth moved into place by ancient glaciers

glacier: a large body of ice and snow that moves slowly over land

immigrant: a person who moves into a foreign country and settles there

peninsula: a stretch of land almost completely surrounded by water

Pilgrim: one of the early English settlers who sailed to Massachusetts in the 1600s. The Pilgrims were seeking the freedom to practice their religion.

precipitation: rain, snow, and other forms of moisture that fall to earth

Puritan: a member of an English religious group that followed a strict form of Christianity. Many Puritans left Great Britain during the 1600s because they were not allowed to practice their religion there.

reservoir: a place where water is collected and stored for later use

treaty: an agreement between two or more groups, usually having to do with peace or trade

union: an organized group of workers that works to improve conditions and wages

INDEX

PHOTO ACKNOWLEDGMENTS